You Can't Cook a Poem Like an Egg!

by

Louise Taylor

edited by
Louise Larchbourne

Copyright © 2015: Louise Taylor

All rights reserved

ISBN-13:9781500630072
ISBN-10:1500630071

For Moira

Acknowledgements

I'd like to thank my editor, Louise Larchbourne, not only for her editing, but for all her inspiration, support and friendship. A huge thank you to my friends – Margret Covell for her endless encouragement, excellent mentoring, voice and performance coaching; Jo Green for keeping me in touch with my creative flow and my body; Andy Davis for his humour, paintings and inspired idea for the front cover; Debbie Phillips for always being there for me.
Lynda Kelly and her fabulous photography; The Buttercup Café in Lewes for inspirational space, food and copious cappuccinos; Ali Bishop and Angels with Attitude and all the friends, poets, coaches and mentors that have helped me
on my journey.

My Mother and late Father from whom I inherited my writing, performing and comic timing!

Louise Taylor

At the age of 9, as the result of writing a poem, I decided that what I wanted to be when I grew up was a writer. At 14, I discovered I had a gift for comedy on stage. There followed a very long gap between then and when I started writing creatively again, and it was poetry that moved me back into it, some time in my mid 30s.

It was my career as a PR consultant that opened the doors to writing, not only a range of items from articles to press releases but also comedy sketches and corporate cabaret for the Christmas parties, in which of course I also performed. Writing poetry returned too. I was invited by someone who came to see one of these shows to join the award-winning Chiswick-based St Michael's Players, an 'am dram' company. Some years later, fearing typecasting as a flat-chested spinster because of my natural comic timing, I set off on my journey to free my bosom and soul by writing and performing my own material.

In 1993, when I emerged with my alter ego, Iona Jette, from the wardrobe, I was writing and performing comedy monologues. My then voice coach, Meribeth Dayme, suggested I become more like Shakespeare, and include poetry. My passion for poetry re-emerged. Although Iona got the first word, or rather poem, I have the last, having decided it was time my voice got a word in. We now share the stage, as well as performing solo. I discovered a world of performance poets and began to perform in it.

I've performed at some of the biggest festivals – *Edinburgh Fringe, Henley, London's Comedy* and literary festival *Book Now!*; *Hailsham Arts Festival, Seaford Literary Festival*; headlined at spoken word venues – *Express Excess, The Poetry Cafe, Short Fuse, The Poetry Police, Lewes Poetry*; and performed monologues – *Iona Jette's Guide to Good Orgasm Management and Naked Truth – diary of an artist's muse* – at fundraisers and events – *Brighton Fringe Festival, FSHG* in Seaford, *Lewes Artwave*, and compered for *Redwood Housing Cooperative's Celebration* on the South Bank.

Being Scottish, Iona and I have also colonised the airwaves on BBC, Talkback and London Network Radio. And of course we can be found at parties, salons, cabarets and even health spas.

Such was my passion, I founded 'The Poet's Kitchen' to encourage and coach more poets to emerge from their dusty corners and perform; I compered and also performed. There were workshops to inspire children and young people as well.

A poem will always go to the heart of the matter, transform the global to the personal and make sense of a world that too often rattles the bones of madness. As you would expect, I cover most of life's themes here and those I haven't will be emerging in my second collection.

Iona has no truck with trivia! She confronts life head-on, penning poetry about socks, sex, and stilettos, with bikini-line waxing a close runner in the race for gold. You'll spot Iona's poems, they are mostly laments and littered wi' Scots dialect.

That leaves me to touch upon love, life, death, and rock 'n' roll!

Louise Taylor
Creative Dynamics Arts & Business Company
www.shoutthesun.co.uk

Contents

Bikini Line Lament	11
Body Heat	13
Constantly Waiting	15
Farewell	17
Fergus & the Compost	19
Floppy Flannel Lament	21
Haikus are like Marmite	23
Have you ever been eaten by a poem?	24
Hot Dogs and Hips	26
Leather Bird	28
Love I'm in a muddle	31
Love-Wrapped Cloaks	34
Lust's Lament	36
Pink Stiletto Boots	38
Morning Workout	40
Pint Pot Poetry	42
Questions to ask the Doctor	43
Rush and Blitzen!	44
Sheba	46
Shock Chocolate	47
Shout the Sun	50
Sock Drawer Lament	52
Stranded on a beach	54
The Rubber Glove Blues	56
The Stars, the Moon and Uncle Stan	59
Twisted River	62

You Can't Cook a Poem Like an Egg!	63

Poetry, Creativity and Business

The Light Bulb	66
The Rock 'n' Roll PR Band	69
Switch Off to Switch On! Business Coaching	73
Soft Through the Trees	74

Blogs:
My Creativity Manifesto	75
Why Businesses Need Creativity	77
The Business of Poetry	79

Bikini Line Lament

The appointment's made, you're filled with dread,
so bad is the fear, your legs turn to lead.
You toss and you turn, peer down below,
shout 'bloody hell, I'm nae gonna go!'
Slowly you rise, by the mirror you stand,
put on the top wi' a trembling hand,
then donning the thong you linger a bit,
mutter out loud, 'mmm, does it fit?'

Your profile shrieks back, 'clench in your big bum
and really do something wi' that flabby tum.'
Your gaze travels down, you're filled with despair,
at the sight that now greets you,
when did *that* get there?

You've gazed at the glossies, ken who's wearing what,
talked to your girlfriends about what they have got.
You're really concerned about looking fantastic,
but you're damned by that fringe round your knicker elastic.

It's natural, it's real, look, have a feel,
if it were on my heid, there'd be no need
to colour or crimp, cos it's never limp.
No regrowth split ends, why can't we be friends?

With the bush in between, instead we must preen
in unnatural ways for hot summer days.

I try to relax but it's, which way to wax?
Choose Brazil or New York, why not Glasgae or Cork?
I'm a red-hot mama, not some page three stunner!
This obsession with youth when I'm long in the tooth –
I ask you –
Did Mae West go a plucking?
No she was too busy.

Body Heat

I watch him
stretching, scratching, yawning,
naked,
calling for his socks and then
pulling black briefs over thighs
of sensuous delight.

Tucking himself on the left
or is it the right?
Playful hands
now buttoning his white shirt,
blue jeans, not too tight,
just enough to reveal a body that's been
blissed in the night.
A red jumper I have slept with,
not as often as him,
so I can taste the body heat
in the cashmere weave.
Now he's slipping his neat feet
into brown leather loafers.
Tea is on its way.

Stretching, yawning, humming,
naked, I am waiting for my tea,
pulling his pillow into my arms
to drink the body heat.
In a sensual doze
I smell a rose
on the tray with the tea
by my side.
The covers slip
as I turn and rise
to note with surprise
his mac is gone.
I reach for my tea and sleepily see
it's five past one.
Time to go back to his wife.

Constantly Waiting

Addicts are we to lives of no passion,
always the fear it'll go out of fashion,
keep popping the pills until we are hags,
lugging our stuff in invisible bags.
Will the time ever come when our work's truly done?
Then at last we poor women can start to have fun.

Tear down the veil,
I'm awa' to abseil
into darkness beyond;
of pain we're a' fond,
we're hungry and needy,
of life we're so greedy,
'Can't wait want it NOW!
Disnae matter how.'

Canned voices from hell don't care if you wait.
They're after your money, don't you just hate?
Press one for your life, two for your death,
left constantly waiting, yet all out of breath.

Gimme baubles, beads, eight suits and a frock,
in loathe with maself, my bank I will shock,
make hate wi' that man, the one of my dreams,

tall, mean and moody, rips up my esteem,
mashes my psyche then blackens my eye,
who am I kidding? my whole life's a lie.

Booze is ma friend,
when will the pain end?
I drink till I greet,
canna make ends meet.
Spliff, pop or crack,
in need of a whack,
my spiritual self
stuck on a black shelf.

Hold the front page of life's greater meaning,
the weapon's the deadline; is that me screaming?
Boxed, packed, shrink-wrapped from birth until death.
Left constantly waiting, yet all out of breath.

Farewell

From tiny paws
to curled-up ancient claws,
she's fed and dined,
purred and inclined
on my lap, my sofa and my heart.

Now she's gone for a life apart.

Whiskers twitching, tail at full mast
rubbing my legs as she wanders past,
curled up asleep.
As I now sit and weep,
remembering the time
when her body was fine.

We conversed in feline speak!
My daily chatter, her miaowful squeak,
Tins and biscuits, litter and oh the poo!
The routine's the same no matter what I do.

Omega left a while ago.

Now Alpha leaves,
as autumn mists and so again I grieve,

named the first, but the second to go
of the two sister cats who looked after me.

A sharing of lives and a long history.

For 20 years I loved her purr,
the softness and colour of her calico fur.

A sighness descends;
farewell my friend.

Fergus and the Compost

Climbing the compost that murmured, murmured,
Fergus the Ferret wondered, wondered,
would he ever reach the top?
Would the murmuring ever stop?
Rain dribbled down the heap.
It was very, very steep,
not full of things asleep,
but murmuring, murmuring,
half eaten birds,
fearsome fly turds.

Fergus the Ferret
took off his wee beret,
fanned away the smell:
'Och I dinna feel well!
I'm awfu' lost
on this heaving compost!'

'In search of something mate?'
said a grubby worm, fishing bait.
'Aye!' Fergus replied
and sighed.
'Somewhere to kip.'
'Well you'll slip

down this heap
if you sleep
here,'
wriggled,
giggled
the worm.
'Head for the garden shed
and you'll find a bed.'

The compost kept murmuring, murmuring,
as Fergus the Ferret
donned his wee blue beret.

Then he slipped.

Floppy Flannel Lament

I'm a wee floppy flannel
that's been flung upon the floor,
full of fluff and bits of stuff.
Ye ken the sort I'm sure.

I'm used by a' the family,
occasionally the dog.
There's soap and spit, hair and shit,
och, that should be in the bog.

I've rubbed around their smelly toes,
wiped big fat hairy oxters,
mopped salty tears, waxed up ears,
that kit beneath their boxers.

I've swished and lathered bouncy bits
on budding blooming girlies,
lathered backs, and bottom cracks,
felt their tirlie mirlies.

I've limply lain on a tum
that wobbles when you breathe,
squeezed pimply spots, caught nasal snot
that showers you when you sneeze.

I've been up and down so many legs,
arms, necks and shoulders too,
'neath grimy nails, in weewee trails,
'cross hands that smell of poo.

There is a place this floppy cloth
has never ever been –
it's hard and square, please put me there!
Aye – the washing machine.

Haikus are like Marmite...

I cannot haiku;
it leaves me without a clue
as to what I can

Have you ever been eaten by a poem?

It will nibble at your ears,
kiss your nose,
fill your eyes with tears,
erode your fears,
cause a fart of smelly smiles.

It will riffle,
ruffle,
snuffle,
through your hair,
cause you to stare,
into the middle distance,
as your mind moves into idle
from overdrive,
thinking you're alive,
yet within you're
parched,
starched.

If you've never been eaten by a poem
it will sip,
sup,
sandwich you up,
'til you feel

your own heart beat,
your soul
sighing for its way.
It's a wonderful sunny day,
but have you noticed?

Hot Dogs and Hips

Brain in a fog
so I ate a hot dog,
saw a chip on my shoulder
the size of a boulder – flicked it off.

Doggone! Where to, damn it?
Not left a note.
Put on my Hush Puppies,
an old afghan coat,
went walkies and whistled,
how much is that doggy in the window?
Trod in a dog's dinner!
Christ I must get thinner!
The state of my hips,
they're like two bulldog clips.

I poodled along.
Big Ben began to bong,
I remembered that song
about mad dogs and men
who should stay in when
it's the middle of the day.

This curtailed my fun,
bloody midday sun!
I ate potato skins,
I'll never get thin!

Dog tired! Stressed! High wired!

Fancied fish and chips,
then remembered the hips.
Spotted a Dalmatian –
or was it an Alsatian?
Felt hounded all day.

Paws for thought.

Are puppy dog tails
as expensive as snails?

Fancied ice cream and chips.
A guy whistled at my hips.
I tipped him a wink.
He turned lobster pink.
Bought yoghurt instead!

Leather Bird

Black leather skirt riffed over my hips,
slinking it on I felt my memory slip
to the drumbeat of the Yardbirds.
Bobbed my head to peer at how high
the pelmet lay across my thighs,
that hadn't seen daylight
since that party when I stripped.
Tried the zip.
Breathed in but not out.
Shall I cry?
Or simply sigh?
'Too tight! Too old!'
my reflection began to shout.

'No! Don't tug it lower! You're my bird!
We're going out!'
sang my man to an Elvis croon.
'So don't follow the herd tonight,
and wear it with thick bloody tights.'

Years of cellulite collided with nude 10 denier.
To a Meatloaf hymn they shouted their presence.
Do I need a year of massage?
Or is there some essence

one can take for thighs
which have lurched to outsize?

'You look gorgeous!
Come here my lovely Leather Bird!'
sang my man to a Pink Floyd paean.
Jiving on the jacket, I'm cleavage aware.
'Hmm!' he hummed,
a makeshift mike in one hand.
'Don't button up bird, I like them to stare.'

Stepping into the stilettos I felt my pelvis shifting.
Paused to wonder just how many of my bits needed
lifting.
Tits, bum, the eyelids
and that chin forever drifting.
'Love you bird!' he rock 'n' rolled
and gave me a squeeze.
I muttered and blenched again
at the state of my knees.
Turning round on a Rolling Stones cloud,
I stared with Stevie Wonder,
at the frontal bulge bursting zipper,
his denim shirt so tight,
I began to ponder
if it and he would last the night.

Grinned at his belly toppling
towards the wrinkly winklepickers.
'Let's head off, Leather Bird
for a blitz of rock 'n' roll!
Life's taken its toll,
our bodies with it,
But the music has our spirit!'

Love I'm in a Muddle!

I'm deeply confused;
change that to bemused
by a man In a van In the country.
I've not got a clue
about what to do
with a man In a van In the country.

What does he feel?
Will this ever be real?
Some things that he said
scurried into my head.
I stirred them around.
There was nothing profound.
Now why am I bound
to a man In a van In the country?

I'm in need of release,
sanity and peace;
I could run and hide,
but something inside
won't let me.

Will the man In a van In the country
be mine for keeps?
I've been waiting for weeks

to see where this goes
and take off my clothes.
Are we lovers or just friends?
When no postcards he sends
why do I feel such a mess?
Perhaps he couldn't care less.
I'm going berserk.
How does Love work?

He's not here but out there.
This just isn't fair!
I don't understand.
Love, give me a hand,
for I really do care
very much
for the man In a van In the country.

I'm very romantic.
He's sounding pedantic.
His voice makes me tingle.
I'm scared; I'll stay single!
Just leave me alone.
But then I will moan
how much I miss
the taste of a kiss,
the feel of a hug.
Do I sound like a mug?

Could do with a cuddle.
Love I'm in a muddle
about how to behave.
Should I be brave?
and use the 'L' word?
Then I'd be absurd
to reveal my heart
when we're always apart,
not together.

I'm no longer confused
or even bemused
by the man in a van in the country.
Love, it's no wonder,
for I'm dating a man
with an Aston Martin Lagonda.

Love-Wrapped Cloaks

Visiting
Dry bones creak in a chair
by her bed – faded eyes look with love in despair
at the wroughtness that has become
her daughter. The nurse wanders in, pill in hand,
stands and looks with uneasiness
at the strain in the room of a woman
half dead, another half alive,
two sisters dressed in red.

They surf the waves
singing,
sighing
laughing,
crying,
watching
the fates unravel the knotted threads
of a life once woven of richness.
Shocked
by the death
of not yet her body,
but her life.
Tortured
by MS.

The nurse returns with the tea –
three cups, a beaker, digestives.
Stands and looks with compassion
at the women in love-wrapped cloaks, telling jokes,
hug-filled stories. Poems of daft delight.
Laughter bandaging their pain.

Departing
One unexpected Sunday morning,
as winter's snow-lit day was dawning,
while they diaried life in normal ways,
trying not to count 'How many more days?'
Of love seeping
hidden weeping,
lightening load
on her uphill road.
Black-cloaked fates sharpened their shears,
severed the years
of suffering and pain.

They're no longer singing, sighing.
Washed ashore where they lie crying,
mourning the loss of a sister,
daughter – Moira's soul flew to the light,
laughed in delight.

Lust's Lament

It began in a mist of the highland kind,
I'd no' seen his face but I loved the behind.
When he turned about I wanted to shout
'Sporrans and joy I've found my toy boy!'
My eyes they filled with starry dust,
well to be honest I was consumed with lust,
I was feeling as hot as a radiator
on account of the loss of my trusty vibrator.

Came as a gift from a pal of mine,
said she'd no need for two at a time.
I clutched it with glee and rushed to my bed,
opened the instructions and carefully read
which way it should go, was it this way or that?
Switched it on and discovered the batteries were flat.

I decided of course this was a temporary measure,
and it widnae be lang afore a man would me pleasure,
not this cold plastic thing with various speeds,
but jings we lassies do have needs,
that must be met.
Och I can tell you've nae used one yet.

It would lie in my handbag all covered in fluff,
next to the lippie and the used powder puff,
so when moments arrived when libido was high,
I'd nip to the loo and let rip with a cry.
Then along came the man with the pretty behind,
so young I was sure he'd have one thing in mind,
but we blethered and supped afore I could get him on hame,
jings was I desperate to get him alone!
How the lusty do fall when they're driven by haste,
I really should have checked my pace,
I tripped over something brought in by the cat,
and landed, no dignity, flat on the mat.

As I lay there feeling all foolish and hurt,
he slowly began to unbutton my skirt,
I started to moan 'just a little bit lower,
and really there's no need to go any slower',
as he tenderly rubbed my badly bruised shin,
he muttered aloud, 'This should go in the bin.'
I looked down beside me to the cause of my fall,
and lying right there on the mat in the hall,
was my cat's wee trophy, Och! How I do hate her,
'twas the battered remains of my trusty vibrator.

Pink Stiletto Boots

Do my knees
look good in these?
Do they lift my bum?
Flatten my tum?
Or just make me
look damn sexy?

I love the pink,
what do you think
I should wear with these?
Move your eyes from my breasts!
Should I wear the pink vest?
That matches the thong
I'm about to put on?

Long skirt or short?
Oops now I've caught
my nails in the
stocking I'm donning.

Would you do up my bra?
Mmm, now move your mouth

just a little to that spot, ah!
Hey! You're supposed to be dressing me,
not suppressing me
up against your firmness.
Do that with your tongue again
and you'll end up in traction!
Take no more action!
My wild woman's in her stride.

Lie back on the bed,
hands over your head,
while I tie them with
black silk stockings.
Shall I stand on the chair?
Slide my hand down there
and softly – No! Wait!
I just don't believe
that you've fallen asleep
yet again!

Morning Workout

I have a longing for tea,
to wipe the sleep from my eyes,
and drift back into a dream.
But I'm swept away by your arousal.
Warm sweat trickles down,
muscles soft from sleep.
This may be your morning workout,
but do I have to shout
about my need
for a cup of tea?

You're alert.
While I'm inert.
I watch the clock,
notice your sock
on the floor,
sigh with relief,
as you roll over.

'Mmm', I say in mock
delight,
'would I be right
in thinking
that now you'll make some tea
for me?'
There's a grunt,
then a snore.
Passions begin to fade.
I make a note to buy a teasmaid.

Pint Pot Poetry
for
Oliver's Poetry Evenings at The Lewes Arms

Slowly sip the sound
of poetry in a pint pot
hang on every word
as it slurps burps
commaless
punctuated sounds
of rhyme and staccato rhythm
crisps and nuts
chomped with a limerick
snacking on a haiku
sonnet by your side
add a tonic
to the epic froth
of a frivolous
performance poem
a sound bite of life.

Questions to ask the Doctor

Can you put a plaster on my fear?
Would you x-ray my anxiety
and tell me who's living there?

Will you hug my shock?
Stroke it gently and listen
to the block
in my state of mind?

Would you give me a pill that makes me feel real?
Instead of one that takes its toll,
masking me as a drug doll?

Can you ask my soul
if it's ready to be healed?

My leg's feeling better.
But the rest of me's elsewhere.

Rush and Blitzen!

It's a quarter to Christmas Eve,
waiting for the night nurse to leave,
clean out of tissues so each time I sneeze
I wipe my nose on my dressing gown sleeve.

Who diaried this date?
When you cannot be late,
trolley dash in Tesco's,
dodging them in Waitrose,
shoved by heaving crushes,
mixed with bright red blushes.
It's a frantic dash,
you're out of cash,
all rush and blitzen,
you're stuck in the kitchen!
There's only one more day,
please move Christmas to May!

It's done!
But Christmas won!
Now the silver tinsel's tarnished
I smell of pudding and garnish;
the scales damn it have to be lying,
husband's got man flu, thinks he's dying,

kids are all bored and feisty,
I'm never out of my nightie,
my blood pressure's rising,
it's hardly surprising
that I've shopped
til I dropped
on line
and the card I used
wasn't mine!

Sheba

Baby cheeks brush my own,
purred fur runs over my chest,
amber eyes seize the day
and a small paw touches my face,
while tiger teeth
nibble my nose
to tell me she's here
and waiting for food.
Cat bonding and life
takes a new turn,
as shredded curtain
climbing frames become
entertainment. Switch off
the TV and switch on
channel kitten at play.

Shock Chocolate

Shock chocolate!
A ball of delight
that wombles and shreckles
and heckles your mind
into blind
submission,
then without permission
you're in a spacecraft.

                                            You'll go to pot
                                                     a lot
                                            if you're not…..

                    where was I?

left in the state
of hallo let's wait
until something happens
                    it never will
                                      but this beats
                                        being still
and it's cheaper than Château Lafite.

I had a moment of wonder,
    then I went under
        an illusion and lost…..
                now what did I lose
            and why did I choose
                to take shock chocolate?

        It's organic,
        don't panic –
        that makes it fine,
        it's juicy and dark
        and the mix is a lark
        of substance abuse
        and chocolate misuse
and when you open your mouth
    world peace is ordained
        but not maintained.

                It took my mind away
                and began to stay.
                Pass a safety pin,
                The gremlin's
                come in

and I'm a baked bean
who's never seen
life outside of the tin!

At what time did I die
and why

did I take shock chocolate?

Shout the Sun
(for Liam, aged 11)

When life is tough
and full of stuff
not wanted,
scheme a dream!
Hullabaloo!
Yip yap!
Rip rap!
Twist and shout!
There'll be no doubt
you'll win through.

When you're stuck
in a rut
with a belly
full of jelly
that turns you inside up,
take a drop of joy,
become your favourite toy.

Leap and lark
from dawn til dark,

look up not down,
be the clown.

Wander barefoot in the sand,
feel the fun inside your hand!
Plick pluck it,
tuck it
under your chin,
take a break,
be a snake,
wiggle your toe,
then let go!
Shout the sun!
Be your fun!
Sparkle star on the beach,
nothing is ever out of reach.

Sock Drawer Lament

My socks are into swapping
and I'm hopping mad.
They start life happy matching pairs
and when I'm not looking,
in the kitchen cooking,
they begin to have affairs.

Where once there was a comfy couple,
pink spots with green,
now there are mismatches
that just have to be seen.
Look! A dayglow yellow
now in touch,
far too much
with a ripened red and golden stars,
found them snuggled up inside my bras.

There's a black 'n' blue twosome
whose patterns are quite gruesome,
found them buried in my knicker drawer.

I can't keep score

of who's with whom
and is there room
for the wee socks
that may result
from this orgy in my underwear?

Imagine the pattern
that'll be reproduced
if the smart black stripes
should seduce
a purple Minnie Mouse.

They don't seem to care
when I turn up and stare
pondering,
wondering
which pair
to wear.
It's too embarrassing,
this colour harassing.
I'll wear tights instead!

Stranded on a beach

Stones beneath her feet.
She listens to a harmony of waves.
Sighing signalling heat of the day.
One woman in a folding chair
sits reading her retirement,
her attention dancing between
the rising tide and safety.
While I struggle with despair,
sunshine mingles with my fear
of being stranded on a beach.

Lulling waves wash over me,
taking me deeper.
One stone beckons me.
I hold it in my hand and listen
to the dancing wind.
I hear its voice:
'Reach behind the despair
to a hidden door
in another place
of enlightenment.'

'Darkness dampens nothing.
It illuminates
a need for soul growth.'

Picking up her folding chair,
she climbs the peak of stones.
Stranded in her retirement,
heading for tea and scones.

While I search for a smile,
sunshine mingles with my release
of no fear
of being stranded on the beach.

The Rubber Glove Blues

I've got the rubber glove blues!

Washing dishes won't make news.
I've hoovered and I've dusted.
Now the dishwasher's busted.

I've got the rubber glove blues.

Hitched to the kitchen sink,
I used to be dressed in mink,
satin basque, stilettos too –
Och, ma Asda pinnie's new.
Hang on, must just stir the stew
and refill my sherry glass
while I wonder if my arse
can clench enough to fit
into a Chanel knit.

I've got the no-sleep bleary-eyed blues.

Changing nappies won't make news,
I'm frazzled frowned & smelly,
sick necklets, floppy belly,

I've got the no-sleep bleary-eyed blues.

Handcuffed to hubbie's wallet
that sticks inside my gullet –
is this trout or red mullet?
I'm nae good at cookin'.
Once I was good lookin'.
All day long it's nappy shit,
leaky boobs & other bits.
Walked the bairns; fed the dog,
now I'm stuck here on the bog,
grabbed a moment for a pee
while they're glued to kids' TV.
Sat here wi' ma sherry glass
and no paper for my arse.

I've got the hormones are raging, just given birth blues.

Our sex life won't make news.
Comes hame the alpha male,
ripe and ready to impale.

I've got the hormones are raging, just given birth blues.

Tho I can still fake a moan,
I want to be left alone,
for ma body's nae ma own.
Switch on the bloody telly
and hide the KY jelly,

put the bairn to my breast,
complain I've had no rest,
pour out a double gin,
pray his footie team will win,
then he'll switch to Channel Five
and start to come alive.
I shall have to find my cap
wi' the bairn in my lap.
I canna tak' nae more –
Hush! Do I hear a snore?

I've got the rubber gloves, no-sleep, bleary-eyed,
hormones raging, just given birth blues.

The Stars, The Moon and Uncle Stan

I stood up.
Counted the stars again.
One was missing,
somewhere in the Milky Way.
Now who had moved it?
Or why had it moved itself?
A mystery.
One I wasn't sure
I could solve easily
without help.
So I turned to the moon,
curtsied and asked permission
to ask a question.

The moon didn't pause
in her ebbing, flowing,
rising and setting;
movement graceful
between new and full.

I stood and waited,
humming a little tune,
tapping my foot.
Not in impatience,
but to the rhythm.

For I never hum from my head,
but from the soles of my feet.
Feeling the rhythm running up
through my belly, my heart and out of my mouth.

Today the tune was a little different,
as I was puzzled
about the star.

Eventually the moon answered.

'You will find the star
in a different position.
It's not disappeared.
It's risen
in the firmament.
It twinkles more brightly
and more often.
You must be still
and at ease
to find it;
preferably smiling
and filled with joy.'

I thanked the moon,
bobbed another curtsey
(though I did wonder
why I needed to).

Now I knew exactly where to find Uncle Stan.

Twisted River

A twisted river flows,
it knows
the way.
Warmly wriggles
over bare toes.
Speeding flows
wash stony beds.
Tossing, roaring
torrents soaring
up fishermen's legs.
Wade in
to shouts of delight,
at childhood swims
in summer light.
A twisted river flows,
it knows
no end.

You Can't Cook a Poem Like an Egg!

Ingredients

- ❖ Words, freshly laid in your heart's hearing; ensure they're free range
  not stopped by the glottal of mundane life
- ❖ Freshly squeezed passion
- ❖ An abundance of ideas
- ❖ Emotions – a pint or two
- ❖ Sprinkling of commas
- ❖ Teaspoon of full stops
- ❖ Time measureless
- ❖ One laptop or PC
- ❖ Notepad and pen

Preparation:

Close the door,
switch off the mobile
and yesterday's unfinished tasks.
Remove the mask of doing, doer,
sit carefully and comfortably,
undisturbed,
fresh tea, coffee, a glass of wine to hand.
Caution: keep the critic out of The Poet's Kitchen.

Instructions:

Pour ideas into your creative bowl.
Crack open the words and stir gently.
Pour in emotions engaged in memories.
Add a smidgen of colourful vocabulary
tho' this isn't always necessary.
Mix, taste, adjust.
Leave to stand.
Sip tea,
stand, stretch, have a pee!
Dream and drift,
as you sift
these first stirrings.
Go walkabout!
Listen to the cat purr; count raindrops,
ponder, reflect but remember,
you can't cook a poem like an egg.
Let it simmer in the slow heat
of your unconscious mind.
Return.
Sieve cold commas, fruity full stops,
exuberant exclamation marks, one or two will do.
Read.
Now carefully lay your mixture
on to your laptop or PC.
Set at one and half line spacing.

It is now in need of some correction,
stirred by your laid-back reflection;
type, delete,
ignore being neat.
It is now in need of more correction,
stirred by your critic's interjection;
type, delete, try being neat.
Use butter-greased verse cutters.
Stifle the critic's mutters.
Save.
Turn down the flame of your inspiration.
Hungrily print out,
smothering the doubt
that your poem is half baked.
Read.
Nod sagely, sip dregs of wine.
Relax.
You know you've cooked your poem.
Serve with no garnish, just as it is.

Poetry, Creativity & Business

As a performance poet I attend events and compose and perform poetry as a memento. For Nick Williams' Inspired Entrepreneurs Community 1st Birthday Party, I composed and performed **The Light Bulb** *from the post-it note creative contributions from Community Members and their guests.*

The Light Bulb

It all began in the glowing serendipity in happy custard.
An intuition filtered through.
'Oh Warrior be switched on
by the brilliant golden illumination
of the freedom and flexibility
that the big "aha moment" brings.'

I dropped everything
as the sun shone on the water,
illuminated incandescence.
I strove to stay triumphant and keep on moving.
My soul somersaulted
and a voice said:
'It's filamental my dear Watson.'
'No it's not,' I replied. 'It's LED.'

'It's a wind of changing tides,'
whispered the light-bulb man and disappeared.
But not my fear.

My heart went ping,
then it went ding,
as I resisted,
yet the knowledge persisted,
insisted,
that I could be the light of the world.
Yet I experienced a bubbling sense of enlightenment.
Then doubt hit me.

Nick's voice, bright on the inside and the out, said:
'When the light goes on start dancing.'

I shook my head.

'Oh, but I feel like a flower opening for the first time.'

Took a sip,
champagne bubbles of inspiration
tickled my nose
and I thought:
'We all need inspiring,
young and old,
fearless and bold.'

Still I hesitated.

'We are the creators of all that we see,' grinned Nick.
'Be wired and inspired,' echoed Niki.

'Well,' I considered,
'I have learnt much from my mistakes;
So I think I'll make some more.'
And began to dance with the other dappled blue horses,
jazzing to the summer breeze.
'We are changing history today.
We can no longer hold back,'
they chorused.
As the light bulb beamed
across the ocean of the world,
I realised
the true leader does not look for a job,
she creates it.

It says something of a company and its leader when some 30 years on we're still in touch and having reunions. This poem is in honour of the fun years we all had at Genesis PR, written as a memento of our first reunion.

The Rock 'n' Roll PR Band

Clink, clank, clatter,
the commuter drone;
a yawn, then a moan
inside the glossy Edwardian wood,
warm as a letter in an envelope,
we slope from the lift to our desks,
shouting: 'Mind the cat!'
ginger stripe, white as milk,
no mat.

Clip, tip, tap, patter,
secretarial chatter,
race, shift the pace
to the one word processor,
check the hair,
spread the lippie,
then sigh, release the fret
with the morning's first cigarette
and breathe the aroma
of a half-drunk cappuccino.

Mike, our suited leader,
arrives meeting-bound,
then wanders round,
wafting aftershave, a joke
to poke
at our day's intent
of client business
over serious bent.

Trill, drill, shrill the constant ringing phones,
listening on our elbow bones
to our clients' brief
wanted yesterday!
We mutter 'no way!'
But do our best,
take no rest
except to smell the sun
rifling through the piles
of files
full of press work.

We never shirk,
unless there's lunch
or a journo out to tea,
leaning on the client's fee.
Or nipping to the corner deli
to fill our 'forever struggling to be flat' belly,

dancing through the dust motes
of Marylebone High Street's
traffic notes.

We grow, expand
til we're no longer a rock 'n' roll band
of PR pros,
but an orchestra.
Some stay, some go,
Alison, Lisa, Debbie
Charlotte, Louise, Chrissie,
Jeff, Claire, Debbie C
and me.
How the memory lurches to recall
us all.

Memories walking through the restaurant door,
as we gather together once more,
no longer quite as thin and now we scurry less.
Yet still the same happy band,
wrapped in the warmth of the Genesis thrall,
we call
our younger selves back.
We hug, speed chatter,
wine flows, must natter
with...
but it's

Eat, Speak, Leave,
to rush
for the plush
red carpet thrill,
Jeff's the director, on the bill
at Leicester Square —
it's a film premiere!

Gathered, we gaze at Jeff from afar,
shining on stage, following his star,
but we've been left
feeling quite bereft
of his company
and of ours so was he!
The question remains of if, how and when
We can have another reunion!

Switch Off to Switch On!
Creative Business Coaching Workshops

My inspiration knew no bounds when I discovered that poetry and my creative business coaching for women in business made for a happy marriage. *Switch Off to Switch On!*, my signature workshop, resolves important personal and business issues by enabling my clients to open up or nourish their creativity swiftly and with greater ease than the other art forms I use.

We co-create a group poem as the finale to being in the creative space. Everyone contributes a line or a word after some stirring of the creative cauldron and I then compose it:

Here's an example from a Switch Off to Switch On! *Workshop for Elaine Hopkins'* Salon for Inspired Entrepreneurs*:*

Soft through the Trees

I have been left, bereft, ill at ease

in winter's work.

Buried.

Now lifting my green leaves and branches

into the cooling breeze,

I feel my buds ready to gently unfold.

White clouds are passing floating to the seas,

as sunlight shines through the fibre of my leaves;

showing them naked.

The first day of spring is soft through the trees.

My Creativity Manifesto

I believe that creativity can illuminate our individual paths to our authentic self. I believe that creativity is essential to our future and to resolving many of our issues as women in business. Here's my eight-point manifesto:

1. **Creativity is innate within each of us:** it arrives with our birth and after us, others take up our creative legacy.

2. **We can all be creative:** creativity is as much about how we are as it as about what we do.

3. **We can all access our own creativity:** even if it's lain dormant for decades, we can still re-connect to it.

4. **Creativity is powerful:** working with imagination, metaphor and nature enables us to transcend our self-imposed and fear-generated limits.

5. **Creativity is insightful:** it illuminates parts of ourselves hidden from our logical mind.

6   **Our creativity enables us to grow and develop:** it emotionally engages us to our intuition, our heart, and our feminine consciousness, enabling us to act out of love and to step into our authentic self.

7   **Working with our own creativity is safe, fun and revealing:** enough said.

8   **Creativity enables our life to become our best performance:** manifesto over.

Why Businesses Need Creativity

Creativity. It's powerful, personal and present – in all of us. Sadly, many of us leave behind the bold, vibrant, vital force that is creativity when we leave childhood. What often blocks us, leaving our creativity shut down, is that we have forgotten the need to *'view the intuitive mind as a sacred gift and the rational mind as a faithful servant.'* (paraphrased from Albert Einstein's writing: Bob Samples, 1976).

Your intuition, your essential business compass hangs out in your creative mind. If you allow your creativity to open up, 'hearing' those hunches becomes easier and clearer. Creative people are more at ease with the unknown. A fear of uncertainty can cause untold stress and lead to poor decision-making.

What surprises many linear thinkers is that the seeming chaos of the creative process has boundaries. In that chaos there is the intention of creating something and control has to be let go of in the creative space. When I want to write a poem I have to allow my intuitive, metaphoric mind free rein, knowing that with reflection and editing – the boundaries – I will create one.

Resilience is another benefit of creativity; vital in today's climate if you are to meet the challenges that are inevitable in business. Reflection is second nature to the creative mind. All artists know that if they put something to one side and allow the unconscious mind to work on it, the next step presents itself easily. The same applies to business problems and personal development in business. Understanding the benefits of being in the flow versus direct action (feminine/creative thinking vs. masculine/linear thinking) can reap benefits for entrepreneurs and business leaders alike in a rapidly changing world, since it can ease stress and present solutions.

Business skills can be learnt – by our intellect and through experience – but a creative approach to learning any new skill will ensure it is learnt more swiftly and anchored more easily – and involves fun! Which leads to the huge healthy benefits of laughter, for without relaxation your creativity cannot be accessed.

If you want your self and your business to flourish take the time to honour your creativity and remember: **You Can't Cook a Poem like an Egg!**

THE BUSINESS OF POETRY

Poetry is not business and business is not about poetry. Yet as an art form, business can learn much from it. Poetry requires an ability to communicate. Business, too, needs to tell its story in order to market its product and, most importantly, it needs to communicate on a human level to its staff, suppliers, and, last but not least, its customers. Above all, in a hard-hitting economy where the Fear Factor can dominate thinking, businesses must remain creative to maintain a leading edge and have a clear and inspiring vision. Whilst price is always a factor, customer loyalty is not price-led – it is about emotional engagement with a company. Hence performance poetry brings a veritable circus ring of skills from which business can learn.

INTUITION, IMAGINATION AND INSPIRATION

Performance poetry, as the name implies, is written for the stage, not the page. As an art form it is the entrepreneur of the spoken word. It has a freer form, flows, leaps, raps and hip hops. Its style mirrors the mind and emotions of the successful entrepreneur, who must retain the capacity to adjust, adapt, and take risks, to be inspirational and creative. By inviting performance poetry into the arena a company learns not only the value of these skills, but also an ability to articulate with language that emotionally engages rather than distances and dehumanises.

Teeming e-mails and nihilistic twitters, that are mere crumbs from the banqueting table of human communication, ensure that our minds become so cluttered we become discombobulated. In an attempt to decipher at the speed of the web we cease to listen. In fact, we can't.

It has been found that 93 per cent of communication is non-verbal (*Prof. Albert Mehrabian, author of* Silent Messages). Is it any wonder that communication and interaction so easily end up in disarray? All too often, business language can deteriorate into insular jargon, lacking emotional engagement, and even clarity of meaning where it is most needed. Far from motivating staff, it can lead to undermining, blocking the free flow of interaction, inspired management and acknowledgement.

In the business of poetry you learn to eliminate unnecessary fogging words and craft a story with the minimum of words. Its performance provides confidence building and communication skills, since you will need to use your intuition, imagination and inspiration to create it. These are also vital tools in managing the fear factor, focusing on business growth and, most importantly, motivating staff in an economic climate that needs to be seen as challenging, not a case for firefighting.

Listening to a performance poet also fires the imagination. Where we listen from is central to our interactions and dialogue. Listening from our own cluttered minds and anxious focus, we cease to be engaged with the person or people with whom we are in communication. This is why 'Poetry Matters', because without it we cease to dream.

LISTENING, LAUGHTER AND EMOTIONAL ENGAGEMENT

To write performance poetry requires emotional engagement with oneself and others, for its aim is to bring the audience into the world of the poet. It also requires humour, which is a vital tool of successful leadership and an integral part of human nature. By observing life poetically, we can often find the humour in the most banal as well as the most tragic of situations and carry ourselves forward. Laughter is a great stimulator of endorphins. Without it we become stuck in a hamster wheel. The hamster has an advantage over us – it knows it's a hamster and is doing what hamsters do best – running round in circles.

It needs an artist's eye view of the world to see both the minutiae of paperclips and the bigger issues of passion, death and rock n' roll! By learning to view business and its challenges metaphorically and with humour, it becomes possible to focus in an entirely new and revitalised way. A paperclip can be just a paperclip to a business mind. To the creative mind it can inspire new ways of exploring problems, like viewing staff difficulties. It may indeed be a metaphor for clipping words together to ensure that they do not fall by the wayside, but are filled with attention-motivating thoughts. So too, the volatility of markets and downturns might be viewed as existential death experiences from which much can be learnt about leadership.

Through performance poetry the mind is moved from the urgency of the next meeting, sales targets, and profit margins to a place of ease, release and new thinking, moving from the past and the future into the moment to listen in new ways. This is why '**Poetry Matters**', for the moment is all there.

Printed in Poland
by Amazon Fulfillment
Poland Sp. z o.o., Wrocław